PA
4246
.E4
1972

Cop.2

Menander, of
    Athens.

The girl from
    Samos, or, The in-
    laws

2.75

DATE		

The Girl from Samos

The Girl from Samos

or

The In-Laws

by

MENANDER

translated into English blank verse

by

ERIC G. TURNER

UNIVERSITY OF LONDON

THE ATHLONE PRESS

1972

Published by
THE ATHLONE PRESS
UNIVERSITY OF LONDON
at 4 *Gower Street, London* WC1

Distributed by Tiptree Book Services Ltd
Tiptree, Essex

U.S.A. and Canada
Humanities Press Inc
New York

© Eric G. Turner 1972

0 485 12019 4

Printed in Great Britain by
WESTERN PRINTING SERVICES LTD
Bristol

PREFACE

This translation was made for the B.B.C. and was broadcast in a production by Raymond Raikes on Radio Three in summer 1971. I should like to think that a fast moving comedy by Menander might be produced on the stage, so I am glad that the Athlone Press has undertaken to publish it. The opening of the play and rather more than half of the prologue has been written by me, not Menander; so have certain other parts of Acts One and Two. These are places where the papyrus manuscript is entirely torn away. At other places where the manuscript is defective I have cobbled over the bad patches, selecting my own text or reconstructing the Greek as I thought best. The play could not be given without this first aid. The translation aims to give pleasure through theatrical liveliness. For the trimeter passages I have used a five foot English line containing a great deal of foot substitution (*Graece* resolution). An attempt to match line for line has been helped out by the insertion of occasional Alexandrines, or of extra half-lines. Menander's trochaic tetrameters are represented by fourteeners. I have inserted minimal stage directions, in which L(eft) and R(ight) are given from the viewpoint of the actors. But I have not thought it right to usurp the producer's function by laying down how every line should be spoken.

I wish my imaginary producer luck. I am sure he will take pains to see that the play sparkles and dances from the outset. Moschiôn will not be allowed to simper, and the old men will not shout. Chrysis' name should be pronounced *Chreesis*, Parmenôn's and Moschiôn's should both form cretics.

I should like to thank Raymond Raikes for an insight into the practical needs of performance, and for his firm correction of some over-literary tendencies.

January 1972   E.G.T.

CONTENTS

INTRODUCTION

'O Menander, O Life, which of you imitated the other?'

When, not more than a century after Menander's death in 291 B.C., Aristophanes of Byzantium made this double-edged mot, he was using that metaphor familiar to Englishmen from Shakespeare's

> 'All the world's a stage
> And all the men and women merely players.'

His word 'imitated' carried an allusion to a famous ancient controversy about the nature of poetical activity (above all, the creativity of a writer for the theatre). Plato had propounded a brilliant, if erratic, theory that artistic creation was a copy of reality at second hand. Aristophanes took the plain man's side in supposing that it is life at first hand that is imitated. And he turned the tables on the high-brows by his half-mocking, half-serious claim that life may also imitate art.

Aristophanes was of course familiar with theatrical conventions that are strange to us. An audience in Athens would have expected a comedy to be stylized and in verse (and Menander's verse is delightfully flexible, and his language spare and supple). They would have expected the action to be completed within the span of a day; the scene normally to be a street, the two houses in which had doors that creaked audibly when they opened to allow an actor on to the stage; female parts to be played by men or boys; the actors to wear grotesque, over life-size masks (one for each character). The set expressions on these masks made facial movements impossible. A Greek actor could not wink or assist the illusion when asked 'Why these black looks?' But he could and probably did mime with his body and use gesture instead. Did these conventions prevent or assist art to imitate life? The ambiguity of Aristophanes' question blessedly allows either interpretation.

Our age is in a better position to assess the justice of his criticism than any other since that of Justinian, since all copies of Menander were lost in the dark ages. For long scholars had to fall back on makeshifts. They could make guesses about passages (never more than 20 lines long) quoted by other writers. But how should these be handled? St Paul's, for instance,

'Evil communications corrupt good manners'?

From recently recovered originals one might guess that this is not to be taken at its face value as sententious drivel, but was put in the mouth of an unlikely character, as it might be a burglar or a cook, to make a comic point. In *The Girl From Samos* the words of Moschiôn (p. 17) survived independently as a 'quote':

I don't think any
One individual is better at
Birth than any other. If you look at
It rightly, it's the moral man who is
Legitimate, the immoral who is
Illegitimate.

It would be hard to divine that on the stage they are the words of a young man who is ashamed to confess to his own father that the girl next door has had a baby by him, and in consequence is clutching at the straws of contemporary philosophy for support.

The second makeshift was to attempt deductions from the Roman adaptations by Plautus and Terence. The discovery in 1968 by Professor E. W. Handley on tattered papyrus from Egypt of a hundred verses of *Cheat Him Twice*, the Menandrian original of Plautus' *Bacchides*, showed how illusory such deductions might be. Plautus changed the order of events and the emphasis; besides he played the scene for laughs in a way not entirely foreign to 'Up Pompeii'. Menander's thoughtful light comedy, which rarely depends on 'laughter holding both his sides', was not to be recovered that way.

The picture began to change with the recovery of fragmentary manuscripts in the Near East, beginning about a hundred years ago with a leaf of parchment taken from a binding in St Catherine's monastery on Sinai. Some 40 early manuscripts on papyrus and parchment have now been collected, few perfect, but some of them extensive. A papyrus book discovered in Egypt in 1905 by Gustave Lefebvre contains substantial parts of three plays, including most of two acts of *The Girl From Samos*. Another papyrus book was acquired in 1958 by Dr Martin Bodmer, whose library in Geneva has now been bequeathed to the Swiss nation as a scholarly foundation. It contains *The Bad-Tempered Man* complete, the first half of *The Shield*, and Acts Three to Five of *The Girl From Samos* complete together with

2

fair fragments of the prologue and the first two acts. These two last-named plays were not published from this manuscript till 1969 in the editions of R. Kasser and Colin Austin. Since then two additional pieces of *The Girl From Samos* (tiny but valuable) have been identified among the unpublished papyri from Oxyrhynchus in England, and I have used them in my translation. In 1961 the papier-mâché chest-casing of a mummy was taken to pieces in Paris by the late A. Bataille, who recovered from it a number of sheets of a roll of *The Sicyonians* copied less than a century after Menander's death. From Oxyrhynchus have come tattered leaves of a papyrus book, which I put together and published in 1965. This gives some 300 verses of *The Man She Hated*. And of this play the prologue was identified as recently as January 1970 by the Belgian scholar Jean Bingen as he lay ill with influenza, and published by B. Boyaval. Meantime a house on the island of Lesbos which began to be excavated in 1961 has furnished mosaic illustrations of some twelve plays. One shows that scene in *The Girl From Samos* in which Demeas throws out his mistress Chrysis, while the cook looks on.

It would be useless to attempt to give synopses of even a selection of these plays. No procedure would be more likely to suggest that Aristophanes was not only wrong, but was trivial in praising Menander for imitating life. You would not recommend *The Importance of Being Earnest* by recounting the incidents of which it is composed or prove an advocate for opera by such a method. Let it be admitted that in Menander a considerable part in the story is attributed to chance; that a favourite device is a recognition scene in which the true parentage of children put out at birth as foundlings is established; that Menander shows maidens saved from pirates, bold but good-hearted courtesans, scheming slaves (we now know one of these directly in *The Shield*, but he is not a Plautine or Frankie Howerd type); that he uses such incidents as the jealous lover who cuts off his mistress' hair, or the misanthrope who gives permission for his daughter's marriage at the moment of shock when rescued from a well. Now such incidents do of course occur in life. No doubt seas and coasts were unsafe in the fourth century B.C. To a hard-pressed parent an unwanted child was another mouth to feed as well as a pointer to a woman's shame (two reasons which moved Thomas Coram to institute the Foundlings Hospital in Bloomsbury). But these ingredients are not the whole of life or even a large part of it. If there were no more in Menander than this we should agree with those critics who label him an escapist from a world in which Macedonian autocracy had left nothing except his private life to an individual; or even with Sir William Tarn who dismissed Menander's themes and characters as unrepresentative of Athenian society, and forthrightly characterised his plays as 'the dreariest desert in literature'.

But it is an obtuse attitude to treat comedy as source material for history without taking into account what a writer for the stage can do and what his audience expects of him. Let us observe slaves on the stage. There are moments in Menander's comedies when a master decides that a slave is concealing something or deceiving him. To find out the truth he will whip him. But on the stage slaves are not whipped—they get away. The audience would hardly tolerate anything else. In real life they do not get away. Theophrastus describes his *Tactless Man* as one who will recall other instances when a neighbour's slave is being flogged. The description confirms both the fact of flogging and Athenian touchiness. The fact is in any case established by the 'kitchen-sink' mimes of Herondas and by documentary papyri from Egypt.

In this respect, then, the convention makes reality impossible to portray. Yet the relationships of slaves to their masters need not be falsified by this handicap. Indeed, a relationship which is an essential element to the plot may be accepted as a true representation of values. In *The Girl From Samos* Parmenôn can tease and lecture Moschiôn, and the unexpected blow to the jaw that he receives in Act Five is a sign that his master is off balance. The fierce loyalty of Getas to Thrasonides in *The Man She Hated*, or of Daos to his supposedly dead young master in *The Shield* (both non-Greek slaves, incidentally!) are elements essential to the action of these plays.

A similar argument might be appealed to on a question of popular morality. It was a serious matter in fourth-century Athens for the wife or daughter of a citizen to be seduced or violated: so serious that an injured party who caught the culprit *flagrante delicto* and killed him could successfully plead justification in the courts. For this reason Moschiôn's predicament in *The Girl From Samos* is potentially a grave one, and the current attitude allows the playwright to find a neat way out of the psychological impasse reached in Act Five. On the other hand, the popular view found no difficulty in accepting that any child that might be born of the liaison between Demeas and Chrysis was an unwanted encumbrance to its father, to be put out to nurse without more ado. Playwright and audience seem to swallow this, to us, extraordinary fact as nothing unusual: if it really were such, Demeas must have put himself beyond the reach of the audience's sympathy.

4

A writer of comedy is under a necessity to amuse his audience as well as tell a plausible story. He cannot force painful themes on their attention as a tragedian can. Grant only that the tragic tension is there and is not relaxed and audiences will accept wild improbabilities, high-flown language, anachronisms, The God from the Machine, even when served up by indifferent actors. But laughter is a solvent of tension; a serious theme in comedy is harder to put across.

The author must in fact get the audience on his side. And here, contrary to expectation, he will find an ally in the conventions. In comedy certain types of character tend to reappear. They wear masks taken from stock. A swaggering soldier, a servant who arrives on the stage out of breath, a garrulous cook, his assistant dragging on a reluctant sheep, children in a nurse's arms: these are tried and tested types, good for effect and for a laugh. The audience knows where it is with them. Better still, a clever author can turn them upside down. Menander does this in *The Girl From Samos* with the stereotypes of father and son—or, more accurately, adopting father and adopted son. It is the 'son' who has persuaded his father to set up his mistress as lady of the house; the father who will constantly find arguments to defend the imagined conduct of his son (conduct which if true would be indefensible). The types are successfully inverted because the audience cottons on. And Menander is thereby able to study seriously the 'terrified affection', to adopt Max Beerbohm's phrase, felt for each other by a father and son who in their relations with others are not timorous at all. It is also dramatically useful to play on the reactions of a bourgeois audience by embodying them on the stage in the attitude of Demeas' neighbour, Nikeratos. This device gives a tart reality to the absurd quarrel between these two contrasted types in Act Four. Moreover, every situation that has confronted Demeas recurs to confront Nikeratos, and our recognition of the echoes in words and action heightens our pleasure.

The relationships in this comedy ring true. It is indeed in the mutual relationships of characters in the enclosed world of each play that a just imitation of life can be claimed for Menander. The drama develops out of the interaction of the characters on each other. Menander puts them in a situation which is possible though it may be unusual, and the complications are resolved by their effect on one another. The world is an enclosed one, but the audience recognises that it is not insulated from life. The more the element of chance is restricted to the early stages (that is, forms part of what is given), the more the interaction is achieved by what the characters actually say to each other, the longer the suspense is maintained—then the better the comedy, the more convincing the imitation of life. In *The Girl From Samos* the course of future action seems calm and settled when the wedding preparations are set in train at the end of Act Two. At this moment the carpet is yanked from under the feet of the two fathers, and all that follows can be sensed, for all its extravagance and preposterousness, as a true imitation of life.

The scene is a street in Athens, the time between 320 and 310 B.C. The backdrop represents two houses, built on to each other. Each has a front door opening on to the street (the convention is that the door creaks audibly before it opens and someone comes out on to the stage). That on the actors' right, the larger house, belongs to DEMEAS; the smaller house on the actors' left is that of NIKERATOS. Between the houses, against the wall, is an altar of Apollo, and behind it a pillar capped by a cone which stands for the god himself. The side entrances to the stage lead on the actors' left to the market place and harbour, on the actors' right to the country. All stage directions are given from the viewpoint of the actors.

During the course of the play the time changes from morning to evening.

ACT ONE

MOSCHION. (*Coming out of the large house RC, and addressing the Altar of Apollo*)
Good morning Apollo, guardian of our house,
Grant me my wish that today will turn out well—
My right eye's twitching, so I'm sure it will!
I won a bet last night on Taurôn, my
Molossian beagle— (*Calls*) Are you there, Taurôn?
  (*With a bark Taurôn enters from RC, panting.*)
Yes, Taurôn, I'm hoping that today a mate
For you will come from Thessaly. First thing
This morning our house-man Parmenôn warned
Me. 'Moschiôn', he said, 'a boat's due in
Today from the North. Your bitch for breeding
May be in her.' 'Your ears are to the ground',
I said. 'Go and see. I'm looking forward
To coupling her with Taurôn. You might even
Pick up a crumb of news about my father
And Nikeratos. Ten months they've been
Away, and now—it's six weeks since we heard
From them.' Off he went. If there's news to be
Got from anyone, Parmenôn will worm it
Out of them. Well, Taurôn, I hope your mate's
Arrived. We need more champions like you.
In you go!
  (*Taurôn runs barking into the house RC.*)
  Odd I should think of father.
Why cry over spilt milk? And yet I keep rubbing
A sore place. I *did* do something wrong.
(*Down C*)
Dear audience, I think I could make it
All seem natural if I paint him as he is.
Demeas, I mean. He's not my real father.
The instant he adopted me I dropped
Into the lap of luxury. I remember well
Those childhood days but needn't tell—his kindness
Was done before I'd learned to notice.

9

I was put on the roll with as good rights as any
Son he might have had—although I'm one of the
'Great unknowns', indeed in many respects
Worse than unknown. (We're by ourselves,
You see.) I became a brilliant patron of the arts,
Full of public spirit—and keen on horses
And hounds—my father paid the bills. We had
Enough to help a friend in need. He taught me
To realise what gracious living meant.
And for all this I made a really civilised
Return—I behaved myself.
Then, as things fell out—I may as well
Tell you all about all of us—I've all
The time in the world—he fell head over heels
In love with this pretty girl from Samos.
An awkward situation, but understandable.
He tried to keep it dark, he was ashamed to tell me.
But I caught him out for all his secrecy,
And I worked it out that if he failed
To set up the girl as his mistress, he'd have
To cope with younger rivals for her favours.
I expect he felt ashamed because of me.
I talked him into bringing her to our house.
That was twelve months ago. Now—if she had been
An Athenian citizen, it would have been unwise
Of me. Adopted nephews have no chance against
Sons born in wedlock. But as she was an alien,
I was safe! I mean, the law won't let you
Marry a girl from Samos.
Our *ménage à trois* worked well; Chrysis, the girl,
Had manners as well as spirit. When in
A month or so father had to make his trip
To the Black Sea, he left her in charge of our house;
He left her pregnant too—but that's another story!
The neighbours took to her: old Nikeratos
And his wife, and their daughter Plangôn—
Darling Plangôn! . . . Nikeratos didn't object
At all to the newcomer forming a firm
Friendship with his daughter. If he had, probably
He wouldn't have gone along as father's travelling
Companion (all expenses paid, of course).
It's now ten months since they left. The agent

In Byzantium (that's the place where
His ships revictual) is a tricky customer;
And the climate there doesn't do father any good.
Nikeratos, I've noticed, hates having
To dip into his pocket—unlike me.
I'm a ready spender. But now he'll very
Likely say I've signed away his property
Without authority. Gentlemen, unless you
Help me when I meet my neighbour, I'm for the high jump.
I told you that my girl's mother took a
Real liking to father's mistress. She
Was in their house, or they in ours, all day long.
Especially that time I came in from the country
And found them here with other guests to celebrate
The Adonis festival. The ceremony
Offered lots of fun, as you'd expect
When it's 'Ladies only' night. But *I* took part,
In fact you might say I was a celebrant.
The noise they made kept me wide awake.
They put up ladders leading to the roof, and kept on
Carrying up bowls of mustard, cress
And fennel, and dancing and making a night
Of it in scattered groups. I daren't tell you the rest.
However—no, I'm ashamed of it. Well,
It must come out—and yet I'm still ashamed.
My girl became pregnant. Now you know the sequel
You know what went before. When tackled
I didn't shrug it off. I was the first to
Go to the girl's mother; I promised to
Make her my wife, and I gave my oath to do it,
Just as soon as father's back. The baby was born
A week or so ago, and I've acknowledged it as mine.
But the girl's mother was worried: what
Would happen when her father got back home,
And found a baby? Well, I'll tell you what happened.
Chance had a lot to do with it. It's an
Odd thing, chance. Chrysis too had *her* baby
Just before, but it didn't live. And so
My baby—Plangôn's baby—has been a sort
Of substitute to her. My own old nurse
Has taken charge—it has been breast-fed in
Our house—and now when Chrysis takes it out

Of doors, most people think it's hers. The servants
Know, of course, but there's been very little
Talk. Least said, soonest mended, as they say.
I wonder why our houseman Parmenôn
Has been so long away down at the harbour. I'll take
A stroll along the road and look for him.   (*Goes L.*)
      (*Chrysis, singing, comes out of house RC. She stops singing as she sees
      Moschiôn. She is carrying a baby in her arms.*)

CHRYSIS. He's in a day-dream going down the road.
We'll slip across next door to Plangôn's. It's time
For baby's morning visit. Dear baby, we'll
Knock at mummy's door. She'll be expecting us,
As she does every morning. You'll smile, baby,
Won't you? Children should smile on their mummy.
Here's the door. What's this, though? Parmenôn,
And in a tearing hurry too. He's just met
Moschiôn. I'll stand here a moment and
Listen to what they're saying. Ssh, baby, ssh!
      (*Enter Parmenôn from L.*)

MOSCHION. Did you see father with your own eyes, Parmenôn?

PARMENON. Don't you ever listen? Of course I did.

MOSCHION. And our neighbour too?

PARMENON.   They've arrived.

MOSCHION.   Well done, them!

PARMENON. But you must be a man and put in a word
   At once about your wedding.

MOSCHION.   How can I? I've
   No courage now the moment's come.

PARMENON.   What do you mean?

MOSCHION. I'm ashamed to face my father.

PARMENON.   And the girl
   You've wronged and her mother? Why, you're trembling
   Like a milk-sop!

CHRYSIS.   What are you shouting for?

12

PARMENON. O, Chrysis, were you *there* then, all the time?
    You ask me why I'm shouting? What a joke!
    I want to get the wedding over, to stop
    This youngster crying outside the house next door,
    Putting out of his head all that he swore to do,
    When all that *I* want is to be sacrificing,
    Putting on the garlands, pounding the sesame
    For the cake. Don't you think I've good reason to shout?

MOSCHION. I'll do everything. No need to go over it all again.

CHRYSIS. I believe you, for one.

PARMENON.   And what about Chrysis
    Here, now your father's coming back? Are we
    To let her go on nursing this baby,
    And say it's her own?

CHRYSIS.   Why ever not?

MOSCHION.   Father
    Will rampage!

CHRYSIS.   He'll calm down again. Why,
    My dear boy, he too is desperately in love
    No less than you. Love leads the hottest-tempered man
    To reconciliation double-quick.
    I'd rather bow to anything than put baby
    Out to nurse in some tenement or other,
    Poor little thing.
    I have myself seen poverty, felt hunger,
    Know what it is to have no man in the family
    To look to for protection. I don't want
    That for this child. Why, Moschiôn, you wouldn't
    Want to deprive *your* son of all you've had
    Yourself? Of course you wouldn't. You wait here
    At the door, kiss your father on both cheeks
    And tell him all. Parmenôn, baby and I
    Will alert the others. Parmenôn, get one
    Of the maids to take that cake I promised
    And slip round to Plangôn's. Forewarned is forearmed.
    (Chrysis and Parmenôn go into the house RC.)

MOSCHION. All this good advice is no help at all.
    How shall I broach the subject to father?

I must have an arresting opening line.
How I hate waiting about.
> (*Door RC creaks open: a maid comes out of Demeas' house and goes into that of Nikeratos.*)

                          What's that? Oh, it's only
The door creaking. It's Chrysis sending her
Maid across to our next door neighbour's.
Everything seems to make me jump this morning.
Father must have a waggon-load of luggage,
To take so long. (*Pause*) Oh, I shall choke. When a
Junior conducts a case himself he needs
A friendly jury. I'm too inexperienced
In pleadings such as these. I know—I'll go and look
For a deserted spot and practise like Demosthenes.
It's no routine brief thrust into my hands.
> (*He goes out R. For an instant the stage is empty. Demeas and Nikeratos with slaves and luggage enter L.*)

DEMEAS. You notice the change of climate instantly,
Don't you, Nikeratos? What a contrast
With that miserable place!

NIKERATOS.   Yes: Black Sea:
Coarse old men, fish wholesale, a really
Boring life. Byzantium: all wormwood
And bitters, by God. But here the simple
Brilliant assets of the poor.

DEMEAS.   Dear Athens,
I pray you gain all you deserve, and so
Make us who love our city most truly
Blessed in everything. Indoors with the
Baggage, men, all that lot into the big house there.
> (*Slaves hump heavy loads into house RC and a small bag is carried into house LC.*)

You there, are you paid to stare at me like
A paralytic? In with you!

NIKERATOS.   What I
Found most extraordinary, Demeas,
About the climate there was this: often enough
You couldn't see the sun for days on end.
A thick sea mist lowered over everything.

DEMEAS. Not only that. They have no splendid monuments.
  The natives thought that a bare minimum
  Of light was brilliance.

NIKERATOS.   You've hit it off
  Exactly.

DEMEAS.   To change the subject, what action
  Will you take on that matter we talked about?

NIKERATOS. You mean about your boy's wedding?

DEMEAS.   That's it.

NIKERATOS. I still stick to my view. Let's seize a happy
  Occasion and fix the day for it.

DEMEAS.   You're
  Resolved?

NIKERATOS. I am.

DEMEAS.   So am I, and I was
  First.

NIKERATOS. Call me out to consult after you've
  Been indoors.

DEMEAS.   I will.   (*At the altar*) Apollo, neighbour
  And guardian of my home, all hail! Thanks for
  A safe return, life, health, prosperity!
    (*He goes indoors to his house RC.*)

NIKERATOS. My daughter Plangôn's in luck. Her husband
  Will be rich. And that dreamy youth is really
  As hard as nails. I'll go in now myself.
  High time, too—there are revellers in
  The streets.   (*At the altar*) Apollo, thanks from me as well.
    (*He goes in too to his house LC.*)

END OF ACT ONE

(*A chorus of revellers enters and sings an intermezzo, the words of which have not survived. The song helps to give the illusion that time has passed between the acts.*)

15

ACT TWO

(Door RC creaks open. Demeas comes out. At first he is speaking back through the door. Inside a baby can be heard crying.)

DEMEAS. If Moschiôn returns, say how eager
His father is to embrace him. And yet—
I'm all out of temper. A crying child
And floods of tears! I need to calm my nerves.
I told Chrysis, if she had my child, to
Be sure to put it out for foundling care.
Why couldn't she have done as she was told?
A nice state I'm in to greet Moschiôn.
(Looking R) Why there he is in the distance. I'll count
Ten before I speak.
  (Moschiôn enters from R.)

MOSCHION.   How do the orators
Do it? I haven't practised any of the things
I had in mind. Once I found myself alone
My thoughts switched to the wedding sacrifice,
Planning the guests, escorting the ladies to the
Bridal bath, handing round the sesame cake,
Singing and whistling the wedding song—not a care
In the world. When I'd had enough—Heavens above,
Here is my father. He must have heard. Hello,
Father.

DEMEAS. Hello to you, son.

MOSCHION.   Why these black looks?

DEMEAS. Every reason. I thought I took a mistress,
And I didn't realize it was a wife
I got.

MOSCHION. Wife? I don't know what you mean.

DEMEAS. She's presented me with a son I don't need
At all—a son, she says. But she'll be sent
Packing with it instantly.

MOSCHION.   Never!
16

DEMEAS. What do you mean, 'Never'? You can't expect me
　　To bring up a son—an illegitimate son—
　　To please someone else—that's not like me at all.

MOSCHION. In heaven's name, (*improvising wildly*) which of us is
　　Legitimate, which illegitimate,
　　Once he enters on the human condition?

DEMEAS. You must be joking.

MOSCHION. 　　　　　　　　I'm not by Dionysus,
　　I'm in deadly earnest. I don't think any
　　One individual is better at
　　Birth than any other. If you look at it
　　Rightly, it's the moral man who is
　　Legitimate, the immoral who is
　　Illegitimate, *and* a slave. This is
　　What Diogenes says, bidding us revalue.

DEMEAS. But won't illegitimacy, like forged
　　Currency, turn out to be a handicap
　　To the city that allows it? Bad money
　　Will drive out good. It's a well-known law.

MOSCHION. No, no, no. You're mixing up economics
　　And Natural Justice by accepting such
　　A law.

DEMEAS. 　And you're talking in riddles. But
　　Suppose you advise me to let this—baby
　　Live in our house, won't you be the loser
　　By putting your own prospects at risk?
　　I mean, I adopted you as my son—not this baby.

MOSCHION. I'll lose much more if I don't stand by the rights
　　Of an inarticulate child like this.

DEMEAS. Inarticulate? You should hear it cry.

MOSCHION. I have. I feel a sense of obligation
　　To it. Father, I helped *you* once. Do me
　　A favour now. Agree to let this child
　　Be reared in your house. I'm serious.

DEMEAS. 　　　　　　　　　　　　You're
　　Serious? All right then, I'll agree. Have it

17

Your own way, Moschiôn. And now it's my turn
To broach a serious topic. You're growing
Up. I don't think I'm a good example
To you. You ought to think of marrying.

MOSCHION. I have been thinking of it.

DEMEAS.   You have? That
Shows you're growing up.

MOSCHION.   If I had a bride
Like the girl next door . . .

DEMEAS.   You mean Nikeratos'
Daughter Plangôn?

MOSCHION.   If that's what you were to
Propose, I'd ask your blessing, and suggest
There's no time like the present.

DEMEAS.   But I do
Approve.

MOSCHION.   If you ask me to marry *her*,
I'll say 'yes', and be unhappy unless the
Wedding's at once.

DEMEAS.   Good boy.

MOSCHION.   I *want* to be
Obedient, not merely seem to be.

DEMEAS. Well done!

MOSCHION.   Then you agree?

DEMEAS.   If our neighbours
Will give *their* consent, you'll marry her tonight!
MOSCHION. I hope you'll see that I'm quite serious,
And will help me without asking a lot
Of questions!

DEMEAS.   You're serious! And I should
Ask no questions! I take your meaning, Moschiôn.
I'll run at once to Nikeratos and
Tell him to start preparing a wedding for
Tonight. You can count on *our* household to help.

MOSCHION. What news! I'll take a bath, pour a libation,
   Light the frankincense and fetch the bride.

DEMEAS. No marching orders yet—not till I find
   Out whether our neighbour will grant our wish.

MOSCHION. He won't say no. But of course it would be
   Tactless to go with you. Anyway, I've got to go
   To the harbour to ask about that bitch.
      (*He goes out L.*)

DEMEAS. Extraordinary coincidence! Chance
   Must after all be a Divinity.
   It solves many a problem that's insoluble.
   I had no idea that he had fallen in love
   With her, and there was I racking my brains
   For reasons to persuade him. I didn't
   Even know how to begin. Not that I've
   Any doubt at all about the match. Nikeratos
   And I have known each other nearly forty years.
   We shared black broth on Parnes standing guard.
   Since the late fiasco of our army,
   His property abroad is forfeit
   And he's fallen on hard times. But I've enough
   For two. It's character, not cash, I paid
   Attention to when looking for a likely
   Wife for Moschiôn. No reason why
   I shouldn't have a grandson that I'm proud of.
   I'm ready to face Nikeratos now.
      (*Goes to Nikeratos' door LC and knocks*)
   House boys! House boys!
      (*The door LC creaks open*)
                              Call out your master. I'd like a
   Word with him on a point of mutual interest.

NIKERATOS. (*Nikeratos appears at his door.*)
   Which is?

DEMEAS.   Oh, Nikeratos, my greetings.

NIKERATOS.   And mine
   To you.

DEMEAS.   Tell me, do you recollect
   We fixed no day for the wedding?

19

NIKERATOS. Quite well. Why?

DEMEAS. Moschiôn has been released from an
Engagement elsewhere tonight.

NIKERATOS. Where and when?

DEMEAS. My motto is to get what has to be done
Done quickly. Tonight is free.

NIKERATOS. In what way?

DEMEAS. We could have the wedding now.

NIKERATOS. Out of the question.

DEMEAS. But I've no other business. Or you either.
He could fetch the bride tonight.

NIKERATOS. Heavens above,
What a suggestion!

DEMEAS. You're backing out? I don't like
To speak like this to you, but I have to say it.

NIKERATOS. But
Instant matrimony before one can send
Invitations to one's friends is not
To my taste.

DEMEAS. Nikeratos, you owe me some
Thanks.

NIKERATOS. Eh, Of course!—It would give me special
Pleasure.

DEMEAS. And I knew you were in earnest
Over the match.

NIKERATOS. You may be sure I shan't hang back
If you agree. What's more, I'll beat you to it.

DEMEAS. Sensible man, I'll see you don't regret it.

NIKERATOS. You're speaking as a friend.

DEMEAS. (*Calls*) Parmenôn! Hello,
Parmenôn!

PARMENON. (*Coming out of house RC*) Yes, master?

DEMEAS.   Take a large basket,
Bring us wreaths, an offering for sacrifice,
And sesame. In short, buy up everything
In the market.

PARMENON.   Everything? Yes, I will,
If others leave me anything.

DEMEAS.   Look sharp.
I mean now! And bring us a cook too!

PARMENON. I haven't got one.

DEMEAS.   Hire one.

PARMENON.   Give me the money
And I'll run.
    (*Money passes.*)

DEMEAS.   Aren't *you* shopping yet, Nikeratos?

NIKERATOS. I must just go in first, and—tell my wife,
And then I'll catch up Parmenôn.
    (*He goes into his house LC.*)

DEMEAS.   Persuading
His wife will be an effort for Nikeratos—

PARMENON. (*Aside L*) Not a thing do I know except that these are
    orders.
Not ours to reason why, or waste our time—

DEMEAS. Are you still there, Parmenôn? Run, man, run.
    (*Parmenôn goes out L, with another slave following. Demeas goes
    indoors.*)

END OF ACT TWO

(*The chorus appear and sing a second intermezzo.*)

ACT THREE

(*Demeas comes out of his house RC.*)

DEMEAS. Odysseus on his raft was going strong
    When an unexpected violent storm

21

Blew up out of a clear sky. Such freak gusts
Have oftentimes dismasted and capsized
Sailors at sea. Such a gust has now struck and knocked
Me sideways! In the middle of this marriage
Preparation, and my thanksgiving
That all was going well. I hardly know
If I see straight any more.
 (*Down C, very intimate*)
        Dear audience,
I've come down stage to confide in you,
With an excruciating pain I can't
Describe. Consider the implausibility
Of it, and pronounce whether I'm sane
Or mad. Did I ever get hold of the right
End of the stick, or not? Am I now inviting
Trouble for no good reason at all?
The moment I went indoors, full of
Enthusiasm to press on with the wedding,
I gave the servants a simple explanation.
They had orders to prepare everything needed—
To sieve, to bake, to trim the wedding basket.
We made progress more or less, although the
Speed of events caused some chaos, as you might
Expect. The baby lay unfussed over,
Bawling its head off. In antiphon the women cried
'Flour, please, water, oil, charcoal'. I myself
Helped to see they got them, and happened to
Have gone into our pantry from which I was
Extracting and inspecting stores. I didn't
Come out at once, and while I was inside
A woman came downstairs from the room above
Into the anteroom in front of our pantry.
(We keep our looms there too, in fact it's the way
Upstairs as well as to the pantry.) It was
Moschiôn's old nurse, well on in years. She used
To be a slave of mine before I set her free.
She spied the baby neglected and crying,
And not knowing I was inside, thinking
It quite safe to speak, went up and made those
Noises women make—'What a darling', 'Treasure',
'Where's mummy gone?'—kissed it and dandled it. And
When its crying stopped, 'Dear me', she murmured,

Half to herself, 'It seems only last year
That I was dandling and nursing Moschiôn
Like this.' And then she said—listen to this—
'And now it's Moschiôn's baby I'm holding
In my arms.' Moschiôn's baby! Well!
Then as one of the maids ran past, the nurse called out
And said 'Give the baby its bath! What's come
Over you? Neglect the little one on
His father's wedding day?' Then I heard the maid
Whisper 'Mind what you're saying. The master's inside.'
'Never! Where?' 'In there, in the pantry.' Then
Double forte the maid said, 'Mistress is
Calling for you, nurse', and in a whisper 'Look sharp.
He hasn't heard a word. What luck!' 'My tongue will be my
        ruin',
Said the nurse. And off she rushed I don't know where.
And I—well, I came out of the pantry just
As coolly as you saw me come out of my house
Just now, as if I hadn't heard or noticed
Anything. In the room outside I saw
Chrysis, my girl from Samos, all alone, holding
The baby, giving it the breast. So that it's
Hers is clear, but who the father is, whether
I am or whether—I can't end the sentence.
Gentlemen, I won't speculate, I bow
To your decision, and simply tell you what I heard.
I'm not angry yet. I think I can enter
Into my boy's feelings. I know he was always
Well-behaved before and couldn't have shown
A more filial duty to me. On the other
Hand, when I reflect on those fateful words,
First that they were uttered by Moschiôn's
Own nurse, second she didn't know I could hear;
And third, when I picture my girl dandling the baby,
Deliberately rearing it against
My wishes—I'm driven right out of my mind.
        (*Voices of cook and Parmenôn off L*)
Why, there's Parmenôn coming back from market.
Just the man I need. Hold on a moment, let him take
His cooking party inside to the kitchen first.
        (*Enter Parmenôn and cook, in full speech. Parmenôn interrupts the
        cook.*)

PARMENON. My dear cook, I've no idea at all why you
Are festooned with all those knives. Your tongue by itself
Could bore through anything.

COOK.   Ignorant amateur!

PARMENON. Me?

COOK.   That's how you strike me, God have mercy.
I've only asked how many places should be laid,
How many lady guests you have, what time
You want to dine, whether you need an extra
Waiter, whether the dinner service is big
Enough and the cook-house has a roof, and
Whether everything else is available—

PARMENON. Number one sausage-meat, dear man, that's what
You're making me, even though you don't see it.

COOK. Go and boil yourself.

PARMENON.   You, too, for every reason.
    (*Going up to the door of the house RC*)
This way, inside!

DEMEAS.   Parmenôn! Parmenôn!

PARMENON. Was someone calling?

DEMEAS.   I was.

PARMENON.   Good afternoon,
    Master.

DEMEAS.   Put your basket down indoors,
Then come here.

PARMENON.   God bless you, Sir, I will.
I trust there's nothing wrong.
    (*He goes in RC.*)

DEMEAS. Not a thing that happens—and of the kind I mean—
Could pass unnoticed by him. He has a finger
In every pie.
    (*Door creaks open RC.*)
                        There now, the door's creaking,
And he's coming out.
    (*Re-enter Parmenôn, speaking back indoors.*)

24

PARMENON. Chrysis, give the cook
Whatever he asks for; and for heaven's sake, keep
The old nurse off the wine jars.
  (*Coming out*)
                            What's to do, master?

DEMEAS. What's to do? Come over here away from the door.
Further yet.

PARMENON. How's that?

DEMEAS. Listen to me,
Parmenôn. A flogging is not what I want
To give you, by the twelve gods, no.

PARMENON. A flogging?
Why, what have I done?

DEMEAS. You're concealing
Something from me, but I've found it out.

PARMENON. No,
By Dionysus, by Apollo here at our door,
By Zeus the Saviour, by Asclepius—

DEMEAS. Stop, it's no good swearing. I'm not simply
Guessing.

PARMENON. Surely it can't be—

DEMEAS. Man, look me
In the eye.

PARMENON. I *am* looking.

DEMEAS. This baby,
Whose is it?

PARMENON. Her-rum!

DEMEAS. I repeat the question:
This baby, whose is it?

PARMENON. Chrysis's . . .

DEMEAS. Who is
Its father?

PARMENON. You, she says.

25

DEMEAS.   That's finished you.
You're deliberately deceiving me.

PARMENON. Not I.

DEMEAS.   I know it all down to the last
Detail, and I've discovered the baby is
Moschiôn's, that you are in the know, and
It's because of him that Chrysis is nursing it.

PARMENON. Who says so?

DEMEAS.   Everyone says so. Answer me this:
Are these the facts? I mean that the baby is
Moschiôn's, that you are in the know, and
It's because of him that Chrysis is nursing it.

PARMENON. Yes, they are master, but nobody need know—

DEMEAS. Nobody need know, what do you mean? Give me
A horsewhip, someone—

PARMENON.   No, for mercy's sake.

DEMEAS. I'll have you branded, I will.

PARMENON.   Branded?

DEMEAS.   Yes,
On the instant.

PARMENON.   (*Runs off R.*)   That's finished me . . .

DEMEAS.   Where are you
Off to, you gallows-bird? Grab him, someone
There. O citadel of Cecrops' land,
O far-flung Empyrean, O—
Demeas, what are you shouting for? They weren't
Even your own words—they were Euripides's—
And besides, you're mad to shout. Take a grip
On yourself, bite your upper lip. After all,
It's not Moschiôn who's injured you.
    (*To audience*)
                            This statement
Gentlemen, may seem bold, but it's the truth.
Suppose he did it deliberately,
Or tormented by sex, or simply because

26

He disliked me, he would have maintained that
Insolent frame of mind and shown his colours
As an enemy. But he's made a complete defence
By his enthusiastic welcome to the
Marriage I proposed. So, it wasn't love
As I thought then, that prompted his haste. No.
He wanted to get away from the house and
Escape that *Helen* of mine indoors. Yes,
She's the guilty party. I expect she
Tempted him one day when he'd had too much to drink
And lost control. Young blood and unmixed wine
Make mischief easily, especially
When a young girl's near at hand. It's just not
Credible that a man who has shown self-control
To everyone else should fail in his behaviour
Towards *me*—of course I know that he is
An *adopted* child, not a son of my body; but it's
His character that matters, not his origin.
But this—wench—is a street-walker,
A public menace. Well then? She'll not stay
Here. Demeas, be a man, put affection
On one side, forget your love, and conceal
What's happened as best you can for the sake
Of your son. Throw this handsome Samian girl
Head-first out of your house.
Your reason can be that she chose to rear
Your child instead of putting it out to nurse ·
As she should have done. No explanations!
Grin and bear it, bite your lip. *Noblesse oblige.*
    (*The door RC creaks open. Enter cook. He stands in the doorway.*)

COOK. Shall I look and see if he's here outside
    The front door? Hello there, Parmenôn!
    The man's made a get-away, and hasn't lifted a finger
    To help me—

DEMEAS.   (*Rushing past him into the house RC*)
               Out of my way, you blockhead.
    (*The door slams.*)

COOK. Phew! What's this? A madman with grey hair
    Has dashed indoors. What can be up? Phew!
    He must be mad, quite mad. Shouting his head

Off, too! My casseroles are lying unpacked
Inside. It would be charming of him if he
Trampled them to smithereens.
(*The door RC creaks open.*)
                              The door is creaking again.
(*Demeas leads out Chrysis with the baby, and the nurse follows. The baby is crying.*)
Damn and blast you, Parmenôn, for bringing *me*
To such a place.
(*He moves to L.*)
                    I'll stand over here out of their way—

DEMEAS. Are you deaf? Get out.

CHRYSIS.   Oh dear. Where in the world to?

DEMEAS. To the devil double quick.

CHRYSIS.   (*Crying*)   Poor me.

DEMEAS.   Yes, 'Poor me'.
It's hard to resist a woman's tears. But I'll
Put a stop to your—

CHRYSIS.   My what?

DEMEAS.   Nothing. You've got
The child, the nurse. To blazes with you both!

CHRYSIS.   Because
I chose to keep my baby—

DEMEAS.   Because of that and—

CHRYSIS. And what?

DEMEAS.   Just that.

COOK   (*Aside L*)   That's what the trouble's about.
I see!

DEMEAS. Once rich you didn't learn how to behave.

CHRYSIS. I didn't learn? What do you mean?

DEMEAS.   When first you
Came here to me, let me remind you, Chrysis,
You were wearing a simple frock.

CHRYSIS.   Well?

28

DEMEAS.   I
Was all in all to you, when you were poor.

CHRYSIS. Aren't you now?

DEMEAS.   Don't speak to me. You have your
Things. I'll give you your nurse as well. Get out
Of the house.

COOK.   (*Aside*)   He's furiously angry. I must
Intervene.   (*Aloud*)   Look here, dear sir—

DEMEAS.   Why are *you*
Addressing me?

COOK.   Don't bite me.

DEMEAS.   Another
Woman, Chrysis, will know how to value what
I offer, yes, and make thanksgiving to heaven.

CHRYSIS. What's the matter?

DEMEAS.   You have given *yourself* a son.
That's all.

COOK.   (*Aside*)   He's not bitten me yet, so I'll
Have another go.   (*Aloud*)   Look here, sir, in spite of—

DEMEAS.   (*Approaching the cook*)
I'll break your head if you talk to me!

COOK.   (*Avoiding him and going RC*)
                          Yes, and
Quite right too. There we are. I'm off straight indoors.
  (*Runs into the house.*)

DEMEAS. Chrysis, you have great charm, and you'll find out
Your true worth in Athens now. They're not on
Your level, those women who charge a mere ten
Drachmas a day for attending dinners
And drink themselves to death on unmixed
Wine, or starve, always supposing they can't
Bring themselves to the other course.
  (*He moves towards the door of his house RC.*)
                              You'll learn the
Hard way, like everyone else, and realize
What happiness your folly threw away.

CHRYSIS. *(Moves towards the door RC)* Demeas—

DEMEAS.   Stay where you are.
(He goes in and shuts the door RC. She sobs, so do the nurse and the baby.)

CHRYSIS.   Alas!
What will become of me?
(Enter Nikeratos from the market L, tugging a lean sheep which bleats.)

NIKERATOS. This sheep I've bought will satisfy the ritual
Demands of the gods and goddesses, once its throat
Is slit.
    (Bleat)
        It has adequate blood and gall, good bones,
And an enlarged spleen, which the Olympians want.
    (Bleat)
The tail's left over. It's for me. I'll cut it
Up and send it to my friends for titbits.
    (Bleat. Baby cries.)
Good heavens, what's going on? Can this be Chrysis
Here crying outside my front door? It can't
Be anyone else. . . . Chrysis, what can have happened?

CHRYSIS. I've been thrown out by your good friend, that's all.

NIKERATOS. By whom? By Demeas?

CHRYSIS.   Yes, Demeas.

NIKERATOS. Why?

CHRYSIS.   Because of this baby.

NIKERATOS.   I heard myself
From my women that you chose to keep your baby
And are nursing it. A mad idea! Still,
Demeas is soft hearted—

CHRYSIS.   He is. And he wasn't
Angry at first, but only later on.

NIKERATOS. Just now, in fact?

CHRYSIS.   Yes, he told me to supervise
The arrangements for the wedding; and while
I was up to my eyes, he burst in on me
Like a madman and locked me out.

NIKERATOS.   Black bile!
  Demeas has got black bile! The Black Sea
  Is not a healthy place. Follow me indoors
  To my wife—with this flaming sheep!
    (*Door creaks open LC.*)
                            Cheer up,
  Chrysis, what of it? He'll drop his madness
  When once he starts to think on what he's done.
    (*They all go into the house LC and the door shuts.*)

END OF ACT THREE

(*The chorus sings another intermezzo.*)

ACT FOUR

(*Door of house LC opens. A baby can be heard crying inside. Nikeratos comes out. At first he is speaking back to someone inside.*)

NIKERATOS. You'll wear me to a frazzle, wife. I'm on my way to
    tackle him.
    (*Door shuts.*)
  I'd have paid a fortune for this incident not to have happened.
  We're right in the thick of a wedding and an untimely
  Omen has occurred: a woman thrown out of house and home
  Has crossed our threshold with a baby in her arms.
  Floods of tears, the women in complete uproar. Demeas
  Is a brute. I take the gods to witness, that I will make him pay
  For his tactlessness.
    (*Moschiôn comes in from L.*)

MOSCHION.   Will the sun never set? Night has quite
  Forgotten her proper function. What endless afternoon!
  I'll have to go and have another bath. What else is there
  To do?

NIKERATOS. Moschiôn, good afternoon to you.

MOSCHION.   Is it time
  For us to begin celebrating the wedding? Parmenôn

31

Met me in the town and told me so. Is there any reason
Why I shouldn't fetch the bride now?

NIKERATOS.   Then you don't know what's happened
Here?

MOSCHION. No. What *has* happened?

NIKERATOS.   You may well ask. A really
Nasty scene.

MOSCHION.   For heaven's sake, what is it? I've been somewhere
Else and haven't heard a thing.

NIKERATOS.   Dear boy, it's your father and he's
Chased Chrysis out of the house.

MOSCHION.   Good heavens! What for?

NIKERATOS.   Because
Of the baby.

MOSCHION.   Then where is she now?

NIKERATOS.   Indoors in *our* house.

MOSCHION. What tidings of disaster!

NIKERATOS.   You think so? Then listen to me.
(*They continue to speak together, down L.*)
*The door of the house RC creaks open and Demeas comes out. He is at
first addressing the servants indoors.*)

DEMEAS. If I have to take a stick to you servants I'll wipe these tears
From your eyes. What nonsense has got into you? See that you do
What the cook tells you.
(*The door is closed.*)
                        It really is something to cry over,
I must say. Virtue has gone out of my house. The results
Prove it.
(*He does obeisance at the altar of Apollo.*)
                        Hail, dearest Apollo! Grant our household good luck
To complete this marriage we're now celebrating. Oh yes,
Gentlemen, I *shall* celebrate the marriage and swallow
My spleen. Lord Apollo, keep watch on me lest I betray
Myself to any. Constrain me, lord, to sing the marriage song. In
    my

Present mood it will prove a thankless task. But I've no choice.
She could never come back.

NIKERATOS. (*Down L: ending conversation*)
> After you, Moschiôn. You talk
To him first.

MOSCHION. (*Pushed forward to C*)
> Well, now . . . Father, why are you doing what you're
Doing?

DEMEAS. What, Moschiôn? Tell me, is your question why has
Chrysis gone?

MOSCHION. Yes—

DEMEAS. (*Aside*) They act as if they were a delegation.
Dreadful thought.

MOSCHION. Yes, Father, why has Chrysis gone?

DEMEAS (*Aloud*) It's not your
Business, it's mine and mine alone. (*Aside*) That's nonsense too!
And it makes
Me convinced he is an accomplice in her guilt.

MOSCHION. Pardon?

DEMEAS. (*Still aside*)
Why does he come to me openly to be her champion?
Of course, I suppose he had to.

MOSCHION. What do you think your
Friends will say when they hear the news?

DEMEAS. Leave my friends out of it.
Let *me* act, Moschiôn.

MOSCHION. I can't let you be rude.

DEMEAS. You mean
You'll interfere?

MOSCHION. Yes, I most certainly shall.

DEMEAS. (*Aside to the audience*) Gentlemen,
The climax outdoing in horror all that went before.

MOSCHION. It's wrong to give free rein to anger.

NIKERATOS. (*Backing up Moschiôn*) Demeas, he's talking
Sense.

MOSCHION. Go in, Nikeratos, and tell Chrysis to come out
  Here at once.

DEMEAS.　　　　　No! Let be. Let be, Moschiôn, for the third time.
  I *warn* you. I know all.

MOSCHION.　　　　　All what?

DEMEAS.　　　　　　　　　Don't bandy words with me.

MOSCHION. I'm forced to, Father.

DEMEAS.　　　　　　　Forced to? Am I not to have any say
  Over what belongs to me?

MOSCHION.　　　　　　Grant it me as a favour, then.

DEMEAS. Favour indeed! I suppose you're asking me to quit my
  Own house and leave you two in it? Let me carry on with
  Your marriage. It must be performed if you've got any sense.

MOSCHION. But I do let you. I simply want Chrysis to be there
  Too in the party.

DEMEAS.　　　　Chrysis!

MOSCHION.　　　　　　I insist on it, and mainly
  For your sake.

DEMEAS.　　(*Turning up C to the altar*)
  　　　　　Apollo, lord Apollo, aren't the facts plain and clear?
  I call on you to witness, lord Apollo, mine
  Enemies are in league one with another. Monstrous. I shall burst
  In two.

MOSCHION. What do you wish to say?

DEMEAS.　　　　　　　Shall I tell you?

MOSCHION.　　　　　　　　　　Yes.

DEMEAS.　　　　　　　　　　　　Come here.

MOSCHION. Speak.

DEMEAS.　　　All right, I *shall* speak. You are the father of the baby,
  That I know. I heard it from Parmenôn who's in your secret,
  So don't trifle with me.

MOSCHION.　　　　　How then has Chrysis injured you,
  Seeing the baby's mine?

34

DEMEAS. Then who is the guilty party?
Or is it you?

MOSCHION. And if I am, how is *she* responsible?

DEMEAS. Do you know what you are saying? Have you no finer
feelings?

MOSCHION. Why are you shouting?

DEMEAS. Why am I shouting, you blackguard? What
A question! You take the blame upon yourself and have the nerve
To look me in the face and ask me that? Does it mean you
Have turned absolutely against your poor old father?

MOSCHION. Have I? Why?

DEMEAS. You can stand there and ask me why?

MOSCHION. What I did
Isn't so very wicked. I'm sure thousands of others, Father,
Have done it.

DEMEAS. Bold as brass! Before this audience I put
The question to you: who is the baby's mother? Tell it
To Nikeratos since you don't think it a crime.

MOSCHION. *(Aside to his father)* Oh lord,
To tell *him* makes it one. He will rampage when he finds out.

NIKERATOS. *(Suddenly drawing the same conclusion as Demeas)*
Oh! You downright, utter scoundrel! I'm starting to have
A glimmering of the filthy conduct that's been going on.

MOSCHION. *(Aside)* Here it comes—this *is* the end.

DEMEAS. You get the point, Nikeratos?

NIKERATOS. Of course. Abomination of desolation! The guilty
Incestuous love-affairs of Tereus, Oedipus, Thyestes,
All the great monsters of the past or of the stage, all these
Are put in the shade by you!

MOSCHION. Me?

NIKERATOS. How could you bring yourself
To commit such outrage? Demeas, your cue. Assume
Amyntor's anger and put out his eyes.

35

DEMEAS. *(Aside to his son)* It's your own fault,
Moschiôn, that all is known.

NIKERATOS. Whose person would you regard
As sacred? What deed of shame not dare? And this is the man
To whom I'm to be marrying my daughter! By god, I'd
Rather have Diomnestus—and everyone knows what happened
To him!

DEMEAS. *(Aside to his son)*
You hurt me deeply but I tried to keep it dark.

NIKERATOS. Demeas, you've a slave's nature, not to resent it.
If it were my bed he'd dishonoured, he'd not have had the chance
To harm anyone else—nor would his bedfellow. I'd have been
The first to sell a concubine or disinherit a
Son of mine. By breakfast time there wouldn't have been
An empty seat in the colonnades or the barbers' shops.
'What a man', they would say, 'Nikeratos has shown himself
In just revenge for murder.'

MOSCHION. It's turned into murder now!

NIKERATOS. I class all acts against authority as murder.

MOSCHION. I'm
Petrified—I can't move a muscle.

NIKERATOS. To cap it all, Demeas,
The wicked murderess has taken sanctuary in my
Own halls! I opened the door to her myself!

DEMEAS. Throw her out, I be
You, Nikeratos. Side with me as a true friend, be sinned
Against with me.

NIKERATOS. *(Moving up to go into his house LC)*
It won't stop me exploding when I see her.

MOSCHION. *(Barring his way)* No!

NIKERATOS. How can you look me in the face, barbarian? Le
Me pass.
(Nikeratos rushes into his house LC and slams the door.)

MOSCHION. Father, for justice's sake, listen.

DEMEAS.   I won't hear
A word.

MOSCHION. What happened isn't what you suspect. I'm just beginning
To see what you're driving at.

DEMEAS.   How do you mean, 'what happened
Isn't what I suspect'?

MOSCHION.   Chrysis isn't the mother of the child
She's nursing. She's doing me a favour by saying it's hers.

DEMEAS.   (*Turning*) What's that?

MOSCHION.   It's the truth.

DEMEAS.   Why ever is she doing you a
Favour?

MOSCHION. I don't like to answer—but I'd rather be hanged
For a lamb than a sheep when you hear the real facts of the case—

DEMEAS. You'll kill me before you get it out.

MOSCHION.   The child's mother is
Nikeratos's daughter, I'm the father. I tried to keep
It dark.

DEMEAS.   Explain yourself.

MOSCHION.   That's exactly what took place.

DEMEAS.   Don't
You bamboozle me.

MOSCHION.   When you can check the facts, what good would
Lying do me?

DEMEAS.   None.
    (*The door LC creaks open.*)
                      That's the door.

NIKERATOS.   (*Approaching the house LC*)   Misery! Oh, misery!
What a sight met my eyes as I rushed through my portal,
Maddened, pierced to the heart with unanticipated woe.

DEMEAS. What's he going to announce?

NIKERATOS.   I came on my own daughter—
Giving the baby the breast!

37

DEMEAS. Then it *is* true.

MOSCHION. Do you hear,
Father?

DEMEAS. You're not guilty, Moschiôn. *I* am, suspecting
What I did.

NIKERATOS. It's you I want to talk to, Demeas.

MOSCHION. (*Going L, fast*) I'll
Make myself scarce—

DEMEAS. Courage!

MOSCHION. It's death even to look at him.
(*Exit L.*)

DEMEAS. What's upset you?

NIKERATOS. She was *giving the baby the breast*, that's
How I found my daughter just now.

DEMEAS. Perhaps she was just playing.

NIKERATOS. It wasn't play. As soon as she saw me coming she fainted.

DEMEAS. Perhaps you thought she did.

NIKERATOS. You and your 'perhaps'. You'll be the
Death of me.

DEMEAS. (*Aside*) To think I caused all this.

NIKERATOS. I beg your pardon?

DEMEAS. (*Aside*) It's incredible.

NIKERATOS. My own eyes saw it.

DEMEAS. (*Aloud*) You're short-sighted.

NIKERATOS. That's no argument. (*Moving up LC again*) I'll go back
and—
(*Exit Nikeratos into house LC.*)

DEMEAS. The devil! Half a minute.
He's gone. Now the fat really is in the fire. It's the end.
This discovery will make him rampage. He'll shout his head
Off. He's a difficult brute, and stubborn as they make them.

Fancy my thinking what I thought! Such thoughts are worse than
    murder.
    (*Much shouting heard from within the house LC.*)
Heavens, what bawling. I expected it. He's calling for fire,
He says he'll set light to the baby. I'll see a roasted grandson.
    (*The door LC creaks open. Nikeratos is coming out again.*)
There's the door. The man's a whirlwind. I mean a thunderbolt.

NIKERATOS. Demeas, Chrysis is in league against *me* now.

DEMEAS.   What?

NIKERATOS.   She's
Persuaded my wife and daughter to admit to nothing.
She has seized the baby and says she won't give it up. Don't
Be surprised if I strangle her outright.

DEMEAS.   What, strangle your wife?

NIKERATOS. Yes, don't you see, she's also in the know.

DEMEAS.   Nikeratos,
Please don't.

NIKERATOS.   (*Rushing up LC to go back into his house*)
           I just wanted to tell you first.
    (*Exit.*)

DEMEAS.   Black bile! That's it!
Our neighbour's got black bile. He's dashed indoors. However
    shall
We extricate ourselves this time? I don't ever remember
Being in such a jam. The best thing is, though, to give him
A straightforward explanation of it.
    (*The door LC creaks open. Chrysis comes out with the baby in her arms.
    Nikeratos is in pursuit.*)
                   Lord, that's the door
Creaking again.

CHRYSIS.   Alas, what shall I do? Whither fly? He'll grab
My baby.

DEMEAS.   (*Moving up RC*) Chrysis, this way!

CHRYSIS.   Who's calling?

DEMEAS.   Take refuge in
My house.

NIKERATOS. Stop, runaway, stop!

DEMEAS. (*To the altar*) Dear Apollo, it looks like
Single combat now. Nikeratos, who are you after?

NIKERATOS. Demeas, stand out of my way! Let me get my hands on
That baby to make my womenfolk open their mouths.

DEMEAS. Never.
(*The door of the house RC is opened.*)

NIKERATOS. Threaten to hit me, would you?

DEMEAS. Yes, I would.
(*Hits him, they struggle.*)
Chrysis, make yourself
Scarce!

NIKERATOS. Then I shall hit *you*. (*Hits him with his stick.*)

DEMEAS. Run for it, Chrysis! He's stronger
Than me.
(*During the struggle Chrysis escapes into the house RC with the baby.
The door closes behind her.*)

NIKERATOS. (*Breathless—struggle over*)
You hit me first, I call on the audience to witness.

DEMEAS. (*Breathless*)
And you're taking your stick to a free-born woman and giving
Chase.

NIKERATOS. Twister!

DEMEAS. Twister yourself!

NIKERATOS. Bring out my baby!

DEMEAS. Don't be funny.
It's mine.

NIKERATOS. No, it is not yours.

DEMEAS. Mine.

NIKERATOS. (*To the audience*) Good people, all of you . . .

DEMEAS. Shout yourself blue in the face.

NIKERATOS. (*Turning*) I'll go into my own house
And do in my wife. What else is there?

40

DEMEAS.   That's just as wicked.
I won't allow it. Halt! Stop!

NIKERATOS.   (*Turning back to Demeas*) Don't you raise a hand to me!

DEMEAS. Control yourself then.

NIKERATOS.   Demeas, you do me wrong. I see
Through you, you're in the secret.

DEMEAS.   Then fire your questions at *me*,
And leave your wife in peace.

NIKERATOS.   Has your boy stuffed me full of lies?
Has he, or has he not, been at my daughter?

DEMEAS.   Fiddlesticks!
He'll marry the girl. Things aren't like that at all.
   (*Taking him by the arm*)
                        Take a turn
Up and down here with me.

NIKERATOS.   I'm to take a turn?
   (*They move up and down stage during the next few speeches.*)

DEMEAS.   Yes, regain
Your equilibrium. Tell me, Nikeratos, haven't you heard
In the tragedy how Zeus came down in a shower of gold,
Flooded through the roof, and got imprisoned Danaê with child?

NIKERATOS. The moral?

DEMEAS.   Perhaps one should be prepared for anything.
Ask yourself if you have a leak anywhere in *your* roof.

NIKERATOS. All over. But what has my roof to do with it?

DEMEAS.   Sometimes
Zeus comes in as a shower of rain, sometimes one of gold.
Do you follow me? It's *his* doing. How quickly we've found
The answer.

NIKERATOS.   Are you leading me up the garden path?

DEMEAS.   Not I,
I promise you. Why you're not a bit worse off than Danaê's
Father. Danaê was prized by Zeus, and Plangôn was by—

NIKERATOS. Moschiôn—but he *has* made a stuffed tomato of me.

41

DEMEAS. He'll marry her, never fear. A divinity has shaped
　These ends, for sure. I could name thousands in the streets of
　　Athens
　Who are the sons of gods—and you have to consider your case
　Phenomenal! First of all Chairephon sitting out there
　In the audience—lunches *à la carte* yet never pays.
　Don't you think that sponger is like a god?

NIKERATOS. 　　　　　　　　　　　　　　I suppose he is.
　All right. I've no choice. I'm not going to fight you over straws.

DEMEAS. You're a man of sense, Nikeratos. Over there is Androcles,
　Ever so many years old, making a pretty penny
　With a skip and a jump. His locks are jet. If they were white
　He couldn't die though you throttled him. Doesn't that make him
　　immortal?
　　(*They stop walking up and down.*)
　To be serious. Pray that this conjuncture turn out well,
　Burn incense. Away! My son will come to escort his bride.
　A man of sense will accept what's sent by Necessity.

NIKERATOS. But if I had caught your son at it earlier—

DEMEAS. 　　　　　　　　　　　　　　　Have done!
　Don't provoke yourself! Resume your preparations indoors.

NIKERATOS. Agreed.

DEMEAS. 　(*Going up RC to his house door*)
　　　　　　　And I'll to mine.

NIKERATOS. 　(*Going up LC to his house door*)
　　　　　　　　Agreed.

DEMEAS. 　　　　　　　　　　　You're a man of resource.
　　(*Exit Nikeratos.*)
　And I'm truly grateful to all the gods and goddesses
　That I find there is no truth in what I thought took place.
　　(*Exit Demeas into his house.*)

END OF ACT FOUR

(*The chorus sings the last intermezzo.*)

ACT FIVE

(Enter Moschiôn from L.)

MOSCHION. Just now I was satisfied at being
Freed from blame I hadn't deserved. I felt that
I'd been given quite adequate relief;
But the more I collect my wits and start
To reflect on what has passed, the more I lose
My self-control and grow beside myself
With anger at my father's notion of what
I'd done. If only all were settled with
Plangôn, and I hadn't so many ties—
My oath, my love, familiarity,
Time, all of which have made of me their slave—
He wouldn't have brought an accusation
Of that sort twice over to my face. No,
I'd have gone abroad to Bactria or
To Caria with the foreign legion.
But now, for your sweet sake, Plangôn, I'll make
No self-assertive gesture. It's wrong and
Vetoed by Love, the master of my mind.
Still, this episode should not be endured
Meekly and dishonourably. I'd like
To scare him, in words if not in deeds,
And *say* I'm going abroad. Then he'll beware
Of future cruelty of such a sort
When he sees I don't sit down under it.
    (Parmenôn can be heard off R.)

PARMENON. Zeus, O Zeus, O Zeus.

MOSCHION. Here's just the man I need, precisely in
The nick of time, Parmenôn, crawling home.
    (Parmenôn enters from R.)

PARMENON. By great Zeus himself it's a stupid and
Contemptible action I've committed.
I was not at fault, yet panicked and
Ran from my master. What could I have done
To justify that? Let's analyse my

43

Case. My *young* master seduced a free-born
Girl: the sinner clearly isn't Parmenôn.
She grew pregnant. Parmenôn's not to blame.
The baby was acknowledged, and smuggled
Into our house: *he* was the smuggler, not me.
A girl in our household said she was
Its mother. What law did Parmenôn break
By that confession? None. Cowardly fool,
Then why did you run away? Ludicrous!
Master threatened to brand me. There you are.
It makes no difference whether you deserve
It or not; in either case it's far from
Civilized.

MOSCHION.   Hello, there.

PARMENON.   (*Turning*)   A good evening
To you.

MOSCHION. Drop this fooling and go indoors
At once.

PARMENON. For what?

MOSCHION.   Bring me out a sword, and
A soldier's cloak.

PARMENON.   A soldier's sword?

MOSCHION.   And hurry up.

PARMENON. What for?

MOSCHION.   Quick march. Carry out your orders
In silence.

PARMENON.   What ever's up now?

MOSCHION.   I'll have to
Find a whip.

PARMENON.   (*Going up to door of house RC*)
            Don't. I'm on my way.

MOSCHION.   Look sharp.
   (*Exit Parmenôn.*)
My father will come to me now. Of course
He'll beg me to stay, and he'll beg in vain—

44

Till the right moment comes. When it's arrived
I'll give way to him. All that's needed is
For me to make the scene plausible—which
I'll find hard—however, here we go.
    (*The door of the house RC creaks open.*)
                                        That's
The door, someone's coming. Well, Parmenôn?

PARMENON. I think you're quite behind the times with what's gone
    on indoors.
Your information's out of date, your intelligence is
Poor. You are upsetting yourself and giving way to alarm
And despondency all for nothing.

MOSCHION.   Haven't you brought them, then?

PARMENON. As a matter of fact, your wedding's on. Wine is being
    Mixed, incense burned, the basket trimmed, offerings set aflame.

MOSCHION. You fool, haven't you brought them?

PARMENON.   It's you, you, they're all waiting for.
Are you going to escort the bride? Congratulations.
You've nothing to fear. Courage! What more could you want?

MOSCHION.   Must you
Lecture me, you oaf?
    (*He slaps his face.*)

PARMENON.   Why that, Moschion?

MOSCHION.   Indoors with you,
Double quick, and bring out what I ordered.

PARMENON.   You've cut my lip.

MOSCHION.   Still
Giving me back-chat?

PARMENON.   (*Going up to the house RC*)
                    I'm on my way. I must say, I've won
A fine reward.

MOSCHION.   Jump to it.

PARMENON.   And they really are celebrating
Your wedding.

MOSCHION. Bring me back other news than that.
  (*Exit Parmenôn.*)
  (*To the audience*) My father
Will come now. But just suppose, gentlemen, that he doesn't beg
    me
To stay, but falls in a temper and lets me go—that's an
Alternative I overlooked just now. What shall I do?
Surely he wouldn't, though? But if he does? He might. I really
Shall look a fool if I have to eat my words.
  (*The house door RC creaks open and Parmenôn re-enters.*)

PARMENON. Here you are—
The cloak and sword—take them—

MOSCHION. Give them here.
  (*He puts them on.*) Did anyone indoors
See you?

PARMENON. No one.

MOSCHION. Absolutely *no* one?

PARMENON. No one at all.

MOSCHION. Really! Oh damn and blast your eyes!

PARMENON. Well, soldier, carry on
Marching to your destination then. I believe you're playing
The fool.
  (*Demeas enters from his house RC.*)

DEMEAS. Tell me, where is he? Hello—what's this?

PARMENON. (*Aside to Moschiôn*) Carry on
Marching, quick.

DEMEAS. What's the point of the uniform? What's gone wrong?
Tell me, Moschiôn, are you going abroad?

PARMENON. (*Moving towards house door RC*) See for yourself,
He's *en route* and half way there. He's asked me to say goodbye
To all at home. I'll do that now . . .
  (*Exit Parmenôn.*)

DEMEAS. Moschiôn . . . I love you for your anger and can't find fault.
Your distress at being unjustly accused is natural.
Yet remember, too, at whom you're aiming your barbed darts.
After all, I am your father. I accepted you as mine,

And brought you up. If your life has been cast in pleasant paths,
It was I who gave it you in full measure. For my sake
You should have borne it even if I hurt you, and shouldered some
Of my troubles like a good son. My accusations of
You were unjust. I showed ignorance, error, madness. But
Think of this: I may have wronged others but I tried to shield
You most of all. I kept to myself what I did not know,
Did not flaunt our dirty linen before our enemies.
But now you choose to expose my fault, call witnesses
To testify to my stupidity. I don't deserve it,
Moschiôn. Don't harbour resentment for that one moment
When I went off the rails, and forget all that went before.
There's much more I could say, but I'll pass it by. It isn't right
To obey a father grudgingly. Do it with a smile.
    (*The door of the house LC creaks open. Enter Nikeratos. He is speaking
    back into the house.*)

NIKERATOS. Don't cross me, wife. It's all been seen to—the bride's
        bath, sacrifice,
    Wedding-breakfast and all. If the groom shows up he'll go off
    With the bride. (*Turns.*) Why! What's this?

DEMEAS.   I've no idea what it means.

NIKERATOS. Really, haven't you? A military cloak! The fellow's
    Thinking of going abroad!

DEMEAS.   That's what he says.

NIKERATOS.   What he says!
    He's going to be stopped, seeing he's a seducer, caught
    In the act and self-confessed. I shall arrest you at once,
    Boy, without ceremony.

MOSCHION.   Go on, arrest me.
        (*He draws his sword.*)

NIKERATOS.   You'll always
    Have your joke with me. Put up your sword at once.

DEMEAS.   Put it up,
    For heaven's sake, Moschiôn. Don't provoke him. Put it up.

MOSCHION. All right then, there!
        (*He sheathes the sword.*)
            If that's what you want. You've nagged at me enough.

47

NIKERATOS. Nagged, did you say? Come here!

MOSCHION. Now I suppose you'll put me in irons?

NIKERATOS. Not at all. Open the doors and bring out your bride.

MOSCHION. Are you
Agreed?

DEMEAS.   Carried unanimously!

MOSCHION.   (*As he goes to house up LC*)   If you'd done this at once,
Father, you'd have been spared your embarrassing lecture just
now.
(*The doors of both houses open. From that LC come out Plangôn and her
mother, from that RC come out Chrysis, the nurse carrying the baby,
Parmenôn, the cook, and other servants. They are carrying torches and
wreaths, and range themselves in a festive ring.*)

NIKERATOS. Plangôn, stand in front of me. In the sight of witnesses,
Moschiôn, I give this woman to be your wife, and bear
Your lawful children—and as dowry I bestow all my
Property on my decease—I pray to live a long time yet.

MOSCHION. And I take her to have, to hold, to cherish.

DEMEAS. Now to fetch
The water for the nuptial bath. Chrysis, send your women,
One to carry the bridal urn, another to play the flute.
Ho there, give us torches and wreaths, so that we can all form
An escort of honour.

MOSCHION.   Here they come.

DEMEAS. Bridegroom, wreathe your head,
Don the laurel.

MOSCHION.   Most willingly.

DEMEAS. Favourites, golden lads,
Seniors, men in the prime of life, if you have liked our play
Clap your hands loudly. Dionysus loves to hear applause.
To you, Victory, immortal patroness, we pray, pick
Out our company as winner in your great festival.

THE END